Star-Struck / "Forever"

Songs Collection

FRANCESCA MORAN

AuthorHouse™
1663 Liberty Drive
Bloomington, IN 47403
www.authorhouse.com
Phone: 833-262-8899

This book is printed on acid-free paper.

ISBN: 978-1-6655-6675-9 (sc)
ISBN: 978-1-6655-6676-6 (e)

Print information available on the last page.

Published by AuthorHouse 09/13/2022

authorHOUSE®

Contents

Introduction

"FOR EVER ",

In memory of David Moran
Music and Lyrics by Francesca Moran
Chord writer/ arranger, Ezra Moran

Is a collection of sixteen musical compositions, derived from the poems in the literary work titled "**STAR-STRUCK**", written by Francesca Moran, and also published by Author House.

The songs are named in order as:

1) Velvet, for ever
2) Promise
3) Kiss me
4) Come with me
5) My lasting dream
6) Pretend
7) Remember then
8) Love among the stars
9) To the end
10) Moonlight tango
11) Somewhere in time
12) Adieu/ Farewell - (French and English lyrics)
13) Doucement/Sweetly (English and French lyrics)
14) Farewell Virginia
15) Heading North
16) Boston

a) were completed on December 15, 2021, and notarized on January 5, 2022
b) officially registered by author Francesca Moran and chords writer/ arranger Ezra Moran with the library of Congress Copy Right office on April 2, 2022,
c) Registration approval and Copy Right issuance date April 4, 2022.

From Author Francesca Moran

OF ALL THINGS BESTOWED BY THE LORD ON MANKIND, LOVE IS THE MOST PRECIOUS ONE. IT CANNOT BE BOUGHT, SOLD, OR TRADED. A TIMELESS JOY AND FOREVER LASTING.

LOVE NEVER DIES.

Velvet, Forever

Francesca N. V. Moran, Ezra Moran (grandson)

Piano chords of "Forever' 16 songs collection Francesca Moran and grandson Ezra Moran

"Forever Velvet"

Dmin7 Root position: **D** + F + A + C
(bass notes) (middle C)
1st inversion **:** **F** + A + C + D
(bass notes) (middle C) (treble note)
2nd inversion**:** **A** + C + D + F (all bass notes) - (**SUGGESTED USE**)

E7 Root position: **E** + G# + B + D - (**SUGGESTED USE**)
(bass notes) (treble note)
1st inversion : **G#** + B + D + E
(bass) (treble)
2nd inversion **:** **B** + D + E + G #
(bass) (treble)

Amin Root position: A + C + E + G
(bass note) (treble notes)
1st inversion: **C** + E + G + A (all bass notes – **SUGGESTED CHORD)**
2Nd inversion**:** **E** + G + A + C
(bass notes) (middle C)

G Root position: **G** + B + D
(bass) + (treble)
1st inversion G/B **:** **B** + D + G
(bass note) (treble notes) (**SUGGESTED USE**)
2nd inversion G/D **:** **D** + G + B (all bass notes)

G/B

It is 1st of G **--** **B** + D + G (**SUGGESTED CHORD**)
(bass) (treble)

Piano chords of "Forever' 16 songs collection Francesca Moran and grandson Ezra Moran

Forever Velvet (continued)

C

Root position: **C** + E + G (all bass notes- **SUGGESTED CHORD**)

1st inversion **E** + G + C
(bass notes) (middle C)

2nd inversion: **G** + C + E

F

Root position: **F** + A + C
(bass notes) (middle C)

1st inversion**:** **A** + C + F (all bass notes- **SUGGESTED USE**)

2nd inversion: **C** + F + A
(all bass notes)

Emin

Root position: **E** + G + B

1st Inversion : **G** + B + E (all bass notes—**SUGGESTED CHORD**)

2nd inversion **B** + E + G

F# dim

Root position : **F#** + A + C
(bass notes) (middle C)

1st inversion: **A** + C + F

2nd inversion: **C** + F + A (all bass – **SUGGESTED CHORD**)

G7

Root position: **G** + B + D + F
(bass notes) (treble notes)

1st inversion: **B** + D + F + G
(bass note) (treble notes)

2nd inversion: **D** + F + G + B
(all bass notes – **SUGGESTED CHORD**)

Promise

In memory of David Moran

Francesca N. V. Moran, Ezra Moran (grandson).

PERFORMANCE NOTES: When any rest is indicated in this piece, the performers shall "pause" for any period of time they wish to.

Kiss Me

In memory of David Moran

Francesca N. V. Moran, Ezra Moran (grandson)

♩=132
Dmin
A7
Dmin
Kiss me, my love, for to-mor-row we part a-gain.
A7
Dmin
5
I will be far a-way, Don't know when I'll be back home.
Emin7(b5)
A7
9
Hol-ding you in my arms, kiss me kiss me a-
Dmin
Emin7(b5)
A7
13
gain. That's all I'll bring with me, your me-mo-ry my
Dmin
17
love.

"Kiss Me"

Dmin
Root position: **D** + F + A
1St inversion : **F** + A + D
2nd inversion **A** + D + F (**SUGGESTED CHORD**)
(bass note) + (treble notes)

A7
root position: **A** + C # + E + G (**SUGGESTED USE**)
(bass note) (treble notes)
1st inversion : **C #** + E + G + A
2nd inversion: **E** + G + A + C#
G + A + C# + E

Emin7/(b5)
root position: **E** + G + Bb + D
(bass notes) (treble note)
1st inversion : **G** + Bb + D + E
(bass notes) (treble notes)
2nd inversion : **Bb** + D + E + G (**SUGGESTED CHORD**)
(bass Note) (treble notes)

Come With Me

In memory of David Moran

Francesca N. V. Moran, Ezra Moran (grandson)

Piano chords of " Forever " 16 songs collection Francesca Moran and grandson Ezra Moran

"Come with me"

F Root position **:** **F** + A + C **(SUGGESTED CHORD)**
(bass notes) (middle C)
1st inversion F/A **A** + C + F
(bass note) (treble notes)
2nd inversion F/**C** **C** + F + A (all bass notes)

C Root position : **C** + E + G (all treble notes) (**SUGGESTED CHORD**)
1st inversion **E** + G + C
(bass notes) (middle C)
2nd inversion**:** **G** + C + E
(bass note) (treble notes)

Bb Root position : **Bb** + D + F (**SUGGESTED CHORD**)
(bass note) (treble notes)
1st inversion **:** **D** + F + Bb (all bass)
2nd inversion **F** + Bb + D

My Lasting Dream

In memory of David Moran

Francesca N.V. Moran, Ezra Moran (grandson)

(♩ = 60)
Swing!
A♭6
D dim7 E♭7/D♭ A♭maj7/E
F m7
Thanks for co - ming in-to my dream. You look so young, as we first
4
B♭m7
E♭7
A♭
A♭
D dim7
E♭7
met some fif-ty years a-go. Tears run down your cheeks.., why so my love.
8
B♭m7
D♭/E♭
E♭7(♭9)
D♭/E♭
A♭
Wak-ing up I know you've left this world. Last cold win-ter My heart is ach-ing
13
C7
F m
F m6
D♭/F
C7
F7
B♭7
so... tears well-ing my eyes too... Please wait for me sweet-heart.
18
E♭7
A♭
E♭7
A♭
We shall meet a gain We shall meet a - gain

Piano chords of " Forever " 16 songs collection
Francesca Moran and grandson Ezra Moran

"My lasting dream"

Ab6 : **Ab** (bass) **+** **C** (middle C) **+** Eb + F (treble)
Ddmin7 : **D** + F + G# + B (all bass)
Eb7/Db : **Eb** + G + A# (bass) + Db (treble)

Abmaj7/E- **Eb** + G + Ab (all bass notes) + C (middle C)
Fm7 : **F** + Ab (bass) + C (middle C) + Eb (treble)

Bbm7: **Bb** + Db + F + Ab (all bass notes)

Eb7 : **Eb** + G + Bb (bass) + Db (treble)

Ab: **Ab** (bass) + C (middle C) + Eb (treble)

Ddim7: **D** + F + G# + B (all bass notes)
Db/Eb : **Eb** (bass) **+** Db + F + Ab (all treble)

Eb/ maj 7 (b9):
Root position : **Eb** + E + G + Bb (all bass notes) + D (treble note)
1st inversion : **E** + G + Bb (bass notes) + D + Eb (treble notes)
2nd inversion : **G** + Bb (bass notes) + D + Eb + E (treble notes)
3rd inversion : **Bb** (bass note) + D + Eb + E + G (treble notes)
4th inversion **D** + Eb + E + G + Bb (all treble notes)

C7**:** **C** + E + G + Bb (all bass notes)

"My lasting dream" (continued)

Fm Root :	**F**	+	Ab	+	C	+	D						
1ST inversion			**Ab**	+	C	+	D	+	F				
2nd inversion					**C**	+	D	+	F	+	Ab		
3rd inversion							**D**	+	F	+	Ab	+	C

F6 :	**F**	+	G#	+	C	+	Db		
Db / F:	**F**	+	G#	+	Db				
Bb / 7 :	**Bb**	+	D	+	F	+	Ab		
Eb 7 :	**Eb**	+	G	+	Bb	+	Db		

Pretend

In Memory of David Moran

Francesca N. V. Moran, Ezra Moran (grandson).

F6 Gm7 C7

I pre - tend you're al - ways by my side.

F6 Gm7 C7

I pre - tend you dear - ly hold my hand. E - ven

F6 D7 G7 C7

though I know you're far a - way. Fly - ing a - mong the stars.

F6 D Gm7 C7

Come on now, a - ppear in my dream...

F6 D Gm7 C7

Hold me tight dar - ling, keep me warm. And love

F7 D G7 Gm7

me as you did be - fore. Kiss - ing me

B♭/C F F7 B♭

ten - der ly. Some day my love,

B♭7

Take me a - way_____ with

F6 Gm7 C7 Am7

you. In - to the night, A - mong the stars,___

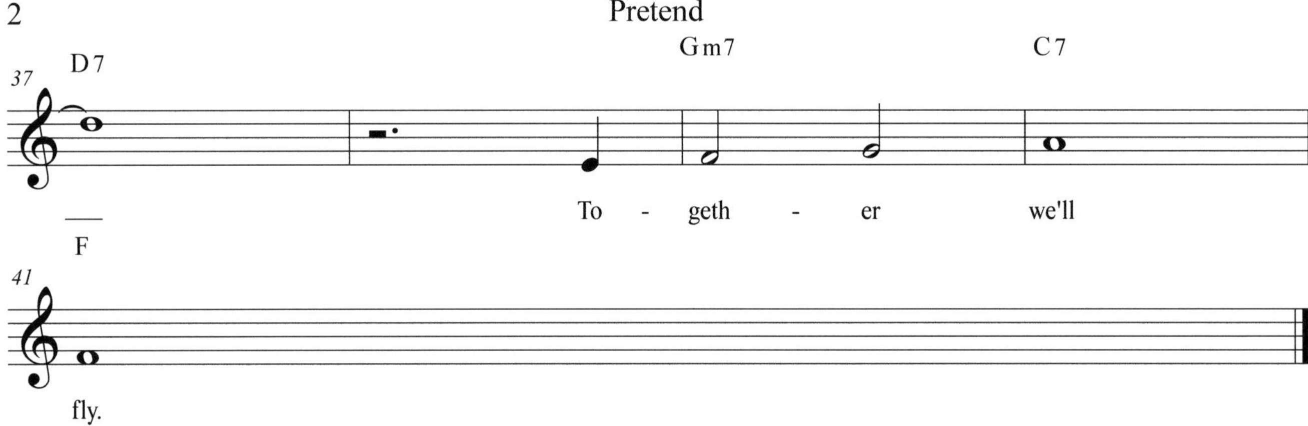
2
Pretend
Gm7
C7
37
D7
To - geth - er we'll
F
41
fly.

Piano chords of "Forever' 16 songs collection
Francesca Moran and grandson Ezra Moran

"Pretend"

F6: root position: **F** + A (bass) + C + D (all treble)
2nd inversion **C** + D + + F + A (all bass notes)

Gm7: Root position**:** **G** + Bb (bass notes) + D + F (treble notes)
2nd inversion: **D** + F + G + Bb (all bass notes)

C7 : Root position: **C** + E + G + Bb (all bass notes)

D7: Root position : **D** + F# + A (bass notes) + C (middle C)

G7 : Root position: **G** + B + D + F (all bass notes)

D : Root position : **D** + F# + A (all bass notes)
1st inversion : **F#** + A (bass notes) + D (treble note)

F7: Root position**:** **F#** + A (all bass notes) + D (treble note)
1st inversion **:** **A** (bass note) + D + F# (treble notes)

Bb/**C** **C** + D + F + Bb (all bass notes)

F Root position**:** **F** + A + C
Ist inversion : **A** + C + F
2nd inversion **C** **+** F + A (all bass notes)

Bb root position : **Bb** (bass note) + D + F (treble notes)
!st inversion **:** **D** + F + Bb (all bass notes)
2nd inversion **:** **F** + Bb (bass notes) + D (treble note)

Bb7 Root position: **Bb** (bass note) + D + F + Ab (treble notes)
1st inversion **:** **D** + F + Ab + Bb (all bass notes)
2nd inversion **F** + Ab + Bb (bass notes) + D (treble note)

Am7 Root position: **A** (bass note) + C + E + G (treble notes) - **SUGGESTED CHORD**
1st inversion **:** **C** + E + G + A (treble notes) - **SUGGESTED CHORD**
2nd inversion **E** + G + A (bass notes) + C (middle C)

Remember Then

In Memory of David Moran

Francesca N.V. Moran, Ezra Moran (grandson)

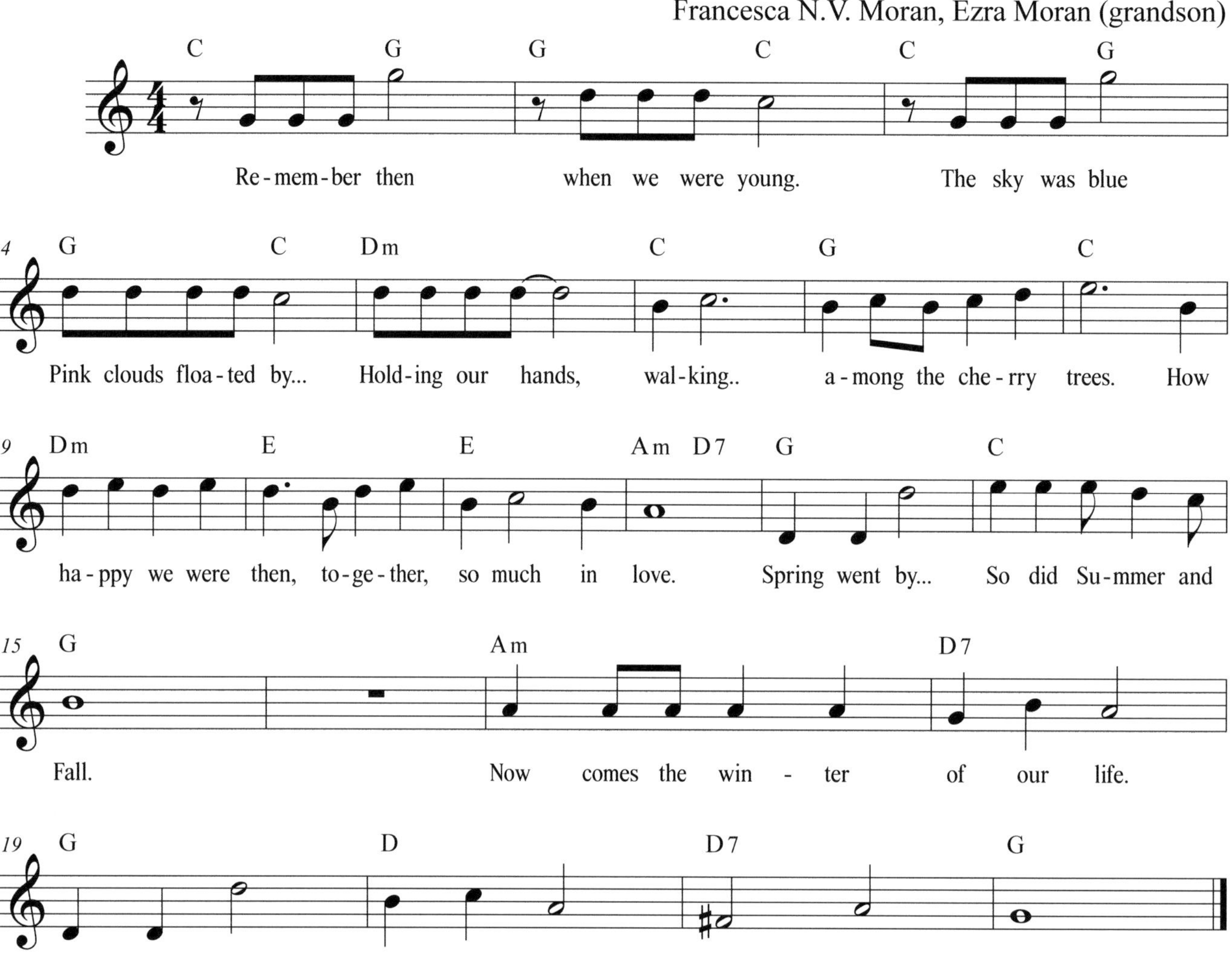
C G G C C G
Re-mem-ber then when we were young. The sky was blue
4 G C Dm C G C
Pink clouds floa-ted by... Hold-ing our hands, wal-king.. a-mong the che-rry trees. How
9 Dm E E Am D7 G C
ha-ppy we were then, to-ge-ther, so much in love. Spring went by... So did Su-mmer and
15 G Am D7
Fall. Now comes the win - ter of our life.
19 G D D7 G
You are gone... and I'm here, all a - lone.

Piano chords of' Forever' 16 songs collection Francesca Moran and grandson Ezra Moran

"Remember then"

C—Root position : C (middle C) + E + G (treble notes)
1st inversion : **E** + G (bass notes) + C (middle C) - **SUGGESTED CHORD**
2nd inversion: **G** (bass note) + C + E (treble notes)

G Root position -- **G** + B (bass notes) + D (treble note)
1st inversion : **B** (bass note) + D + G (treble notes)
2nd inversion **D** + G + B (all treble or bass notes)

Dm Root position -- **D** + F + A (all bass)
1st inversion : **F** + A (bass) + D (treble)
2nd inversion: **A** (bass) + D + F (all treble)

Am --- Root position: **A** (basss note) + C + E (treble notes)
1st inversion **C** + E + A (all bass)
E + A (all bass) + C (middle C)

D7---Root position : **D** + F# + A (all bass notes) + C (middle C)

D --- Root position : **D** + F# + A (all bass notes)
1st inversion : **F#** + A (all bass notes) + D (treble note)
2nd inversion : **A** (bass note) + D + F# (all treble notes)

E : **E** + G# + B (all bass)

Love Among the Stars

In Memory of David Moran

Francesca N.V. Moran, Ezra Moran (grandson)

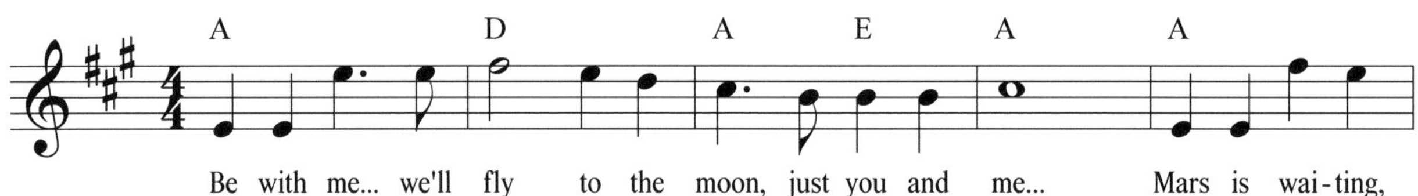
A D A E A A
Be with me... we'll fly to the moon, just you and me... Mars is wai-ting,

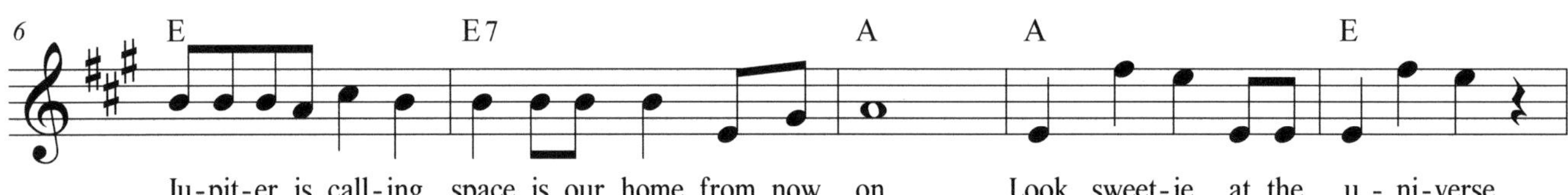
6
E E7 A A E
Ju-pit-er is call-ing, space is our home from now on. Look, sweet-ie, at the u-ni-verse,

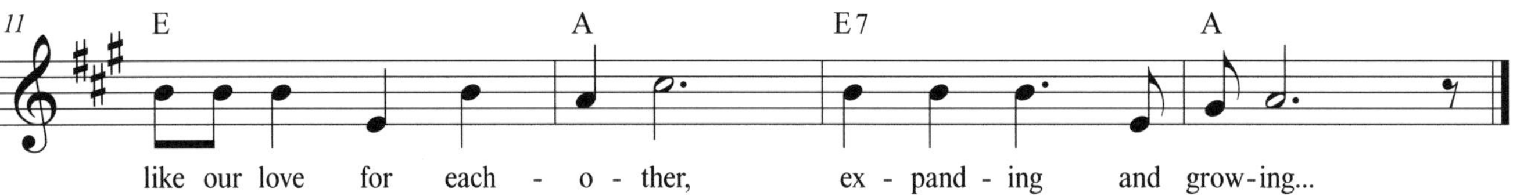
11
E A E7 A
like our love for each - o - ther, ex - pand - ing and grow-ing...

Piano chords of' Forever'16 songs collection
Francesca Moran and grandson Ezra Moran

"Love among the Stars"

A—Root position: **A** + C# + E
1st inversion **:** **C#** + E + A (all bass notes)
2nd inversion **:** **E** + A (all bass notes) + C# (treble note) -- **SUGGESTED CHORD**

D—Root position: **D** + F# + A (all treble notes) – **SUGGESTED CHORD**
1st inversion **:** **F#** + A + D
2nd inversion : **A** + D + F#

E—Root position : **E** + Ab + B (either bass or treble notes)
1st inversion : **Ab** + B (bass notes) + E (treble note)—**SUGGESTED CHORD**
2nd inversion **:** **B** + E + Ab

E7 -- root position : **E** + G# + B (bass notes) + D (treble note)

To the End

In Memory of David Moran

Francesca N.V. Moran, Ezra Moran (grandson)

Piano chords of " Forever' 16 songs collection
Francesca Moran and grandson Ezra Moran

"To the End "

G---Root position : **G** + B + D
(bass notes) (treble note)
1st inversion : **B** + D + G
(bass) (all treble)
2nd inversion : **D** + G + B

D --- Root position : **D** + F# + A
(all bass notes)
1st inversion : **F#** + A + D
(bass notes) (treble note)
2nd inversion: **A** + D + F#
(bass note) (treble notes)

C--- Root : **C** + E + G (all treble)

Moonlight Tango

In Memory of David Moran

Francesca N.V. Moran, Ezra Moran (grandson)

29
E♭/F
B♭
D7
For sure
Ne - ver
Le - tting you go.
My love,
33
G7
Cm7
F7
B♭
lis - ten
to my heart - beat
For
you!

Piano chords of " Forever' 16 songs collection Francesca Moran and grandson Ezra Moran

"Moonlight Tango"

B -- Root position : **B** (bass note) + D# + F# (all treble)
1st inversion **:** **D#** + F# + B (all bass)
2nd **inversion** **F#** + B (bass) + D# (treble)

Bb—Root position: **Bb** (bass note) + D + F (all treble notes)
1St inversion: **D** + F + Bb (all bass)
2nd inversion: **F** + Bb (all bass) + D (treble)

G7—Root position: **G** + B + D + F (all treble)
1st inversion: **B** (bass) + D + F + G (all treble)
2nd inversion**:** **D** + F + G + B (all bass clef)
3rd inversion**:** **F** + G + B (all bass) + D (treble)

C7: **C** + E + G + Bb (all bass)

Eb/F -- **F** (bass) + Eb + G + Bb (all treble)

Eb7/b9—Root position: **Eb** + E + G + Bb (all bass) + D (treble)
1st inversion**:** **E** + G + Bb (all bass) + D + Eb (all treble)
2nd inversion: **G** + Bb (all bass) + D + Eb + E `(all treble)

Eb maj 7: **Eb** + G + Ab + D
4th inversion: **D** + Eb + G + Ab (all bass) - **SUGGESTED CHORD.**

Piano chords of " Forever " 16 songs collection Francesca Moran and grandson Ezra Moran

" Moonlight Tango" --(continued)

Bb6 : inversion: **D** + F + G **+** Bb (all bass clef)

7 (# 9) : **F** + A (bass) + C (middle c) + Eb + Gb (all treble)

D7-- inversion D7/C : **C** + D + F# + A (all bass)

Gm-- Root position : **G** + A# (all bass) + D (treble)

Gm7- Root position: **G** + Bb (all bass) + D + F (all treble)
1st inversion : **Bb** (bass) + D + F + G (all treble)
2nd inversion: **D** + F + G + Bb (all bass) – **SUGGESTED CHORD.**
3rd inversion: **F** + G + Bb (all bass) + D (treble)

F7—Root position: **F** + A (bass) + C (middle C) + Eb (treble)
1st inversion : **A** (bass) + C (middle C) + Eb + F (all treble)
2nd inversion: **C** + Eb + F + A (all bass)
3rd inversion: **Eb** + F + A (all bass) + C (middle C)

Somewhere in Time

In memory of David Moran

Francesca m. v. Moran, Ezra Moran (grandson)

Piano chords of " Forever " 16 songs collection Francesca Moran and grandson Ezra Moran

"Somewhere in time"

G - Root position **:** **G** + B (bass clef) + D (treble clef)
1st inversion**:** **B** (bass clef) + D + G (all treble clef)
2nd inversion: **D** + G + B (all bass clef)

Emin-- **E** + G + B (all bass clef)

Amin: Root position : **A** + C + E
(bass clef) (treble clef)
1st inversion **:** **C** + E + A (all bass clef notes) – **(SUGGESTED CHORD)**
2nd inversion **E** + A + C
(all bass clef) (middle C)

A7—A7/C# inversion: **C#** + E + G + A (all bass clef)

D7 – Root position : **D** + F# + A + C
(all bass clef) (middle C)

B7—Root position : **B** + D# + F# + A
Inversion B7/D# : **D#** + F# + A + B (all bass clef) – **SUGGESTED CHORD**

Adieu/Farewell

In Memory of David Moran

Piano chords of "Forever' 16 songs collection Francesca Moran and grandson Ezra Moran

"Adieu / Farewell"

F – Root position: **F** + A (all bass) + **C** (middle C)
Left hand : 5 + 3 (all bass) + 1 (middle C)--- Right hand : 1 + 3 + 5 (all treble)
1st inversion: **A** (bass) + **C** (middle C) + F (bass)
2nd inversion **:** **C +** F + A (all bass clef**)--** **SUGGESTED CHORD**

Bb – Root position**:** **Bb +** D + F (from lowest notes to highest notes)
1st inversion : **D +** F + Bb (all bass clef)
2nd inversion: **F +** Bb (all bass clef) + D (treble clef) **--SUGGESTED CHORD**

C – Root position**:** **C +** E + G (treble)
1st inversion: **E +** G + **C**
(bass clef) (middle C**)**
2nd inversion**:** **G** + C + E
(bass) (all Treble)

C7 -- Root position :C + E + G + Bb (bass clef or treble clef)
1st inversion C7/E: **E +** G + Bb (all bass) **+** **C** (middle C)
2nd inversion C7/G**:** **G +** Bb (all bass) **+** **C** (middle C) **+** E (treble)
(SUGGESTED CHORD)
3rd inversion C7/Bb : **Bb +** C + E + G **(SUGGESTED CHORD)**

Doucement/Sweetly

In Memory of David Moran

Francesca N. V. Moran, Ezra Moran (grandson)

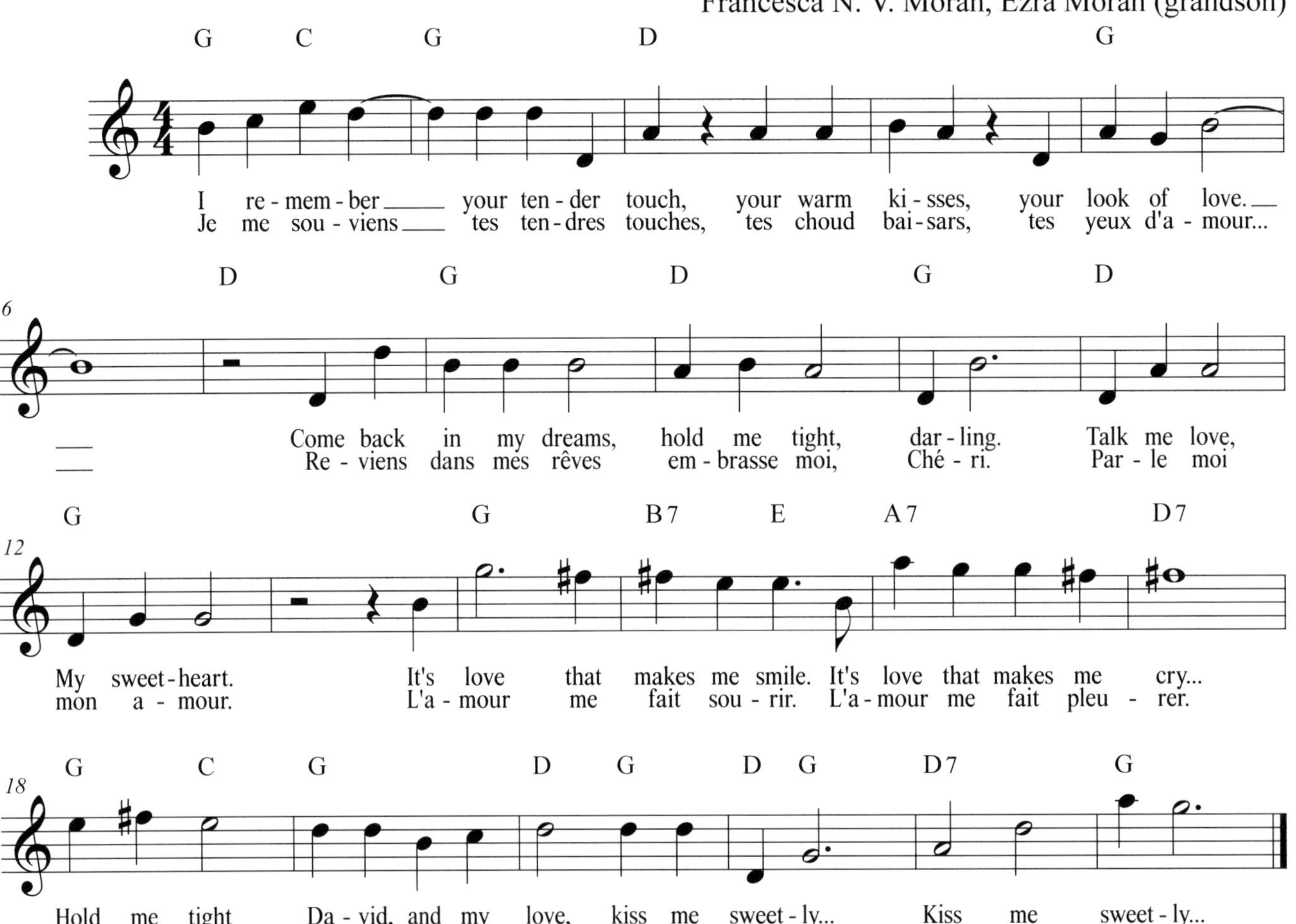
G C G D G
I re - mem - ber your ten - der touch, your warm ki - sses, your look of love.
Je me sou - viens tes ten - dres touches, tes choud bai - sars, tes yeux d'a - mour...
6
D G D G D
Come back in my dreams, hold me tight, dar - ling. Talk me love,
Re - viens dans mes rêves em - brasse moi, Ché - ri. Par - le moi
12
G G B7 E A7 D7
My sweet - heart. It's love that makes me smile. It's love that makes me cry...
mon a - mour. L'a - mour me fait sou - rir. L'a - mour me fait pleu - rer.
18
G C G D G D G D7 G
Hold me tight Da - vid, and my love, kiss me sweet - ly... Kiss me sweet - ly...
Em - brasse moi Da - vid, Do - nne moi un doux bai - ser... un doux bai - ser...

Piano chords of "Forever' 16 songs collection Francesca Moran and grandson Ezra Moran

"Doucement / Sweetly"

G –Root position: **G** + B (all bass clef) + D (treble clef)
1st inversion **:** **B** (bass clef) + D + G (treble clef)—**SUGGESTED CHORD**
2nd inversion: **D** + G + B (all treble clef)

C—Root position: **C** + E + G (either bass or treble clef)
1st inversion **:** **E** + G + C
2nd inversion: **G** + C + E

D—Root position: **D** + F# + A (all bass clef)
1st inversion **:** **F#** + A (bass clef) + D (treble clef) - **SUGGESTED CHORD**
2nd inversion: **A** (bass clef) + D + F# (treble clef)- **SUGGESTED CHORD**

B7—Root position: **B** (bass) + D# + F# + A (all treble clef)
1st inversion: **D#** + F# + A + B (all treble clef)- **SUGGESTED CORD**
2nd inversion**:** **F#** + A + B + D# (all treble)
3rd inversion: **A** + B + D# + F#

E—Root position : **E** + G + B (all Treble) -**SUGGESTED CHORD**
1St inversion : **G** + B (bass) + E (treble)
2nd inversion: **B** (bass) + E + G (treble)

A7—Root position: **A** + C# + E + G
1st inversion **C#** + E + G + A
2nd inversion: **E** + G + A + C#

D7—Root position : **D** + F# + A (bass) + C (middle C)
1st inversion : **F#** + A (bass) + C + D (treble)
2nd inversion: **A** (bass) + C + D + F# (treble)-- **SUGGESTED CHORD**
3rd inversion: **C** + D + F# + A (all bass clef)

Farewell Virginia

In memory of David Moran

Francesca N. V. Moran, Ezra Moran (grandson)

Piano chords of "Forever' 16 songs collection Francesca Moran and grandson Ezra Moran

"Farewell Virginia"

G – Root posiiton: **G** + B + D
1st inversion, G/B: **B** + D + G
2nd inversion, G/D **D** + G + B (all bass)

G+- (G augmented chord or G major chord) :
G + B + D# (all treble)
1st inversion **:** **B** (bass) + D# + G (all treble) - **SUGGESTED CHORD**
2 nd inversion: **D#** + G + B (all treble) -**SUGGESTED CHORD**

EMIN/G: **G** (bass) + B (bass) + E (treble)

G7: Root position: **G** + B + D + F
1st inversion, G7/B ***:*** **B** (bass) **+** D + F + G (all treble)
2nd inversion, G7/D: **D** + F + G + B (all bass)
3rd inversion, G7/F***:*** **F** + G + B (all bass) + D (treble)

C—Root position: **C** + E + G
1st inversion: **E** + G (all bass) + C (middle c)
2nd inversion: **G** (bass**)** + C + E (treble)

Cmin7—Root position: **C** + Eb + G + Bb
1st inversion: **Eb** + G + Bb + C
2nd inversion***:*** **G** + Bb + C + Eb
3rd inversion***:*** **Bb** + C + Eb + G

"Farewell Virginia" (continued)

F7—Root position: **F** + A (all bass) + C + E (all treble)
1st inversion: **A** (bass) + C + E + F (all treble)
2nd inversion: **C** + E + F + A (all bass)
3rd inversion: **E** + F + A (all bass) + C

G/D—inversion of chord G : **D** + G + B (all bass)

D—root position: **D** + F + A (treble or bass clef)
1st inversion: **F** + A + D
2nd inversion: **A** + D + F

Amin7: Root position: **A** (bass) + C + E + G (all treble)
1St inversion : C + E + G + A (all treble)
2nd inversion: **E** + G + A (all bass) + C (middle c)
3rd inversion: **G** + A (all bass) + C + E (all treble)

B7: **Bb** + D + F + Ab

"Farewell Virginia" -- (continued)

E7/G#--- Root position of E/7: **E** + G# + B + D
1st inversion: **G#** + B (bass) + D + E (treble)
2nd inversion: **B** (bass) + D + E + G# (all treble)
3rd inversion: **D** + E + G# + B (all treble)

Eb maj7—Root position: **Eb** + G + Bb + D (all treble clef)
1st inversion: **G** + Bb (bass) + D + Eb (treble)
2nd inversion: **Bb** (bass) + D + Eb + G (treble)
3rd inversion: **D** + Eb + G + Bb (all bass)

Ebmin7-- Root position: **Eb** + Gb + Bb + Db
1st inversion: **Gb** + Bb (bass) + Db + Eb (all treble)
2nd inversion: **Bb** (bass) + Db + Eb + Gb (all treble)
3rd inversion: **Db** + Eb + Gb + Bb (all bass)

Bb7: **Bb** + D + F + Ab

Heading North

In Memory of David Moran

Francesca N. V. Moran, Ezra Moran (grandson)

Piano Chords of " Forever " 16 songs collection
Francesca Moran and grandson Ezra Moran

"Heading North"

F—Root position : **F** + A + C
Left hand 5- 3- 1 Right hand 1- 3- 5
F/A inversion: **A** (bass) + C + F (treble)
F/C inversion: C + F + A (all treble)

C—Root position: **C** + E + G (all treble)
C/E 1st inversion: **E** + G (bass) + C
C/G 2nd inversion : **G** (bass) + C + E (treble)

G—Root position: **G** + B + D
1st inversion : **B** + D + G
2nd inversion: **D** + G + B (all bass)

G7—Root position: **G** + B + D + F
1st inversion : **B** (bass) + D + F + G (all treble)
2nd inversion: **D** + F + G + B (all bass)
3rd inversion : **F** + G + B (all bass) + D (treble)

Boston

In Memory of David Moran

Francesca N.V. Moran, Ezra Moran (grandson)

Piano Chords of 'Forever " 16 songs collection Francesca Moran and grandson Ezra Moran

"Boston"

A—Root position : **A** (bass) + C# + E (treble)
1st inversion: **C#** (middle C#) + E + A (treble)
2nd inversion: **E** + A (all bass) + C# (middle C#)

E—Root position: **E** + G# + B (all bass)
1st inversion: **G#** + B (all bass) + E (treble)
2nd inversion: **B** + E + G# (all bass)

C# m—Root position: **C#** (middle C#) + E + G# (all treble)
1st inversion : **E** + G# (bass) + C# (middle C#)
2nd inversion: **G#** (bass) + C# + E (all treble)

D—Root position: **D** + F# + A (all bass or treble)
1st inversion: **F#** + A (all bass) + D (treble)
2nd inversion: **A** (bass) + D + F# (treble)

C#7—Root position: **C#** + F + G# + B (all bass or all treble)
1st inversion: **F** + G# + B (bass) + C# (middle C#)
2nd inversion: **G#** + B (bass) + C# + F (all treble)
3rd inversion: **B** (bass) + C# + F + G# (all treble)

F#m—Root position : **F#** + A (bass) + C# (middle C#)
1st inversion : **A** (bass) + C# (middle C#) + F# (treble)
2nd inversion : **C#** + F# + A (all bass)

Bm = **B** (bass) + D + F# (all treble)

Printed in the United States
by Baker & Taylor Publisher Services